HEALTH MATTERS

Asthma

Carol Baldwin

Heinemann Library
Chicago, Illinois

©2003 Reed Educational & Professional Publishing
Published by Heinemann Library, an imprint of
Reed Educational & Professional Publishing,
Chicago, Illinois

Customer Service 888-454-2279

Visit our website at www.heinemannlibrary.com

Designed by Patricia Stevenson
Printed and bound in the United States
by Lake Book Manufacturing

07 06 05 04 03
10 9 8 7 6 5 4 3 2 1

Library of Congress Cataloging-in-Publication Data
Baldwin, Carol, 1943–
    Asthma / Carol Baldwin.
        p. cm. — (Health matters)
Includes bibliographical references and index.
    ISBN 1-40340-248-5
    1. Asthma—Juvenile literature. [1. Asthma.
    2. Diseases.] I. Title.

RC591 .B35 2002
616.2'38—dc21
                                    2001007972

Acknowledgments
The author and publishers are grateful to the
following for permission to reproduce copyright
material:

Cover photograph by Laura Dwight/Photo Edit

p. 4 Zefa/Benelux Press; p. 5 BSIP/Jacopin/Science
Source/Photo Researchers, Inc.; p. 6 Jeff Isaac
Greenberg/Photo Researchers, Inc.; p. 7 Science
Pictures Ltd./Corbis; p. 8 Image Bank/Getty Images;
p. 9 Lisa Quinones/Black Star
Publishing/PictureQuest; p. 10 Stone/David
Hanover; p. 11 Damien Lovegrove/Science Photo
Library/Photo Researchers, Inc.; p. 12 Roy
Morsch/Corbis Stock Market; p. 13L Glaxo Smith
Kline; pp. 13R, 25 Custom Medical Stock Photo,
Inc.; p. 14 Trevor Clifford; p. 15 Jose L.
Pelaez/Corbis Stock Market; p. 16 David Young-
Wolff/PhotoEdit/PictureQuest; p. 17 Jeffry W.
Myers/Stock Boston, Inc.; p. 18 Stone/Lori Adamski
Peek; p. 19 Joseph Nettis/Stock Boston,
Inc./PictureQuest; p. 20 Jack Ballard/Visuals
Unlimited; p. 21 Gareth Boden; p. 22 Michael
Pole/Corbis; p. Andrew Syred/Science Photo
Library; p. 24 Geostock/PhotoDisc; p. 26T Neil
Leifer/Sports Illustrated; pp. 26C, 27T
Bettman/Corbis; p. 26B Kit Houghton/Corbis; p.
27C AP Wide World Photos; p. 27B Keith
Srakocic/AP Wide World Photos

Every effort has been made to contact copyright
holders of any material reproduced in this book.
Any omissions will be rectified in subsequent
printings if notice is given to the publisher.

Some words are shown in bold, **like this.** You can find out what they
mean by looking in the glossary.

Contents

Children who have asthma don't have to miss out on activities. With a doctor's help, they can keep their asthma under control and enjoy doing the same things as other children.

What Is Asthma?

The word "asthma" comes from the Greek language. It means "to breathe hard." For people who have asthma, it can be very difficult to breathe sometimes. This is called an asthma attack.

People with asthma can have slightly different **symptoms** during an asthma attack. The main symptoms are:

◆ coughing

◆ wheezing, or noisy breathing

◆ getting short of breath

◆ a tight feeling or pain in the chest

Some people might have only one of these symptoms. It might be a cough that won't go away, or they might feel out of breath sometimes. Other people with asthma might have all of these symptoms.

But having any or all these symptoms doesn't always mean that a person has asthma. It could just mean that they have a cold or an infection. Asthma is a **condition** that stays with a person for a long time.

During an asthma attack

Asthma affects a person's **bronchi.** These are the two tubes that carry air in and out of the **lungs.** During an asthma attack, a person's bronchi become **inflamed,** meaning they become red, swollen, and sensitive. Things like having a cold or breathing in smoke can irritate the bronchi of a person with asthma. The result is an asthma attack.

In an asthma attack, the muscles around the **airways** tighten and the lining inside the airways swells. This means there is less room for air to pass through, and it's harder to move air in and out of the lungs. This makes it difficult to breathe. Sometimes the airways also fill with **mucus.** Airways clogged with mucus can make a person wheeze and cough.

airway before an asthma attack

airway during an asthma attack

During an asthma attack, the lining of the airways starts to swell, the muscles tighten, and mucus may be produced.

Asthma symptoms can be relieved quickly with special medicines. These medicines relax the muscles and reduce swelling in the airways. This makes the airways wide enough for air to pass through again.

5

What Causes Asthma Attacks?

An asthma attack happens when a person with asthma comes in contact with an asthma **trigger.** A trigger is anything that irritates the **airways** and causes the asthma **symptoms** of coughing, wheezing, difficulty breathing, or a tight feeling in the chest. There are many different asthma triggers, and every person with asthma has a different set of triggers that can start an attack.

Many people who have asthma also have **allergies.** An allergy happens when the body's **immune system** reacts to something in the **environment.** People who have allergies have allergic reactions to such things as dust or pets, which do not usually cause reactions in other people. Allergic reactions may include asthma symptoms, or may cause sneezing, watery eyes, a runny nose, or a rash. The substance or thing that a person is allergic to is called an **allergen.**

Doctors have found that some cats are more likely to trigger asthma attacks than others are. That's because some cats shed one hundred times more allergens than others.

The following lists explain the most common triggers for people who have asthma.

Allergy-induced asthma triggers

Molds release tiny **spores** into the air. The spores can trigger an asthma attack in some people if they are breathed in.

◆ Dust mites: These microscopic relatives of crabs and spiders live mainly in carpets, beds, and sofas. Their droppings cause problems for many people with asthma when they are breathed in.

◆ Molds: Molds grow in damp places, both indoors and outdoors. Damp basements, leaf piles, and humidifiers usually contain large amounts of mold.

◆ Animals: Furry or feathered animals such as cats, dogs, and birds can cause asthma attacks in people who are allergic to them.

◆ **Pollen:** Pollen is a fine powder released by flowers, grasses, and trees. Pollen can cause asthma attacks in some people when it is breathed in.

◆ Food: For some people, eating foods such as nuts, milk, eggs, seafood, chocolate, and wheat can cause asthma attacks.

◆ Medicines: Some people with asthma are allergic to aspirin and other similar medicines. Taking aspirin to relieve pain can trigger an asthma attack in some of these people.

Other asthma triggers

◆ Colds, flu, and other illnesses caused by viruses and bacteria: Infections of the respiratory system are common asthma **triggers.** In winter, about eight out of ten children who go to the hospital because of asthma attacks have infections such as colds.

◆ Cigarettes: Cigarette smoke makes a lot of people with asthma cough and feel out of breath. Children who grow up in homes where people smoke are more likely to have asthma.

◆ Strong smells: The smells of paint, glue, perfume, soap, and gasoline can cause asthma attacks in some people.

People who have asthma often can't use perfume because it could trigger an asthma attack.

◆ Sleeping: Some people have no asthma symptoms when they go to bed, but wake up in the middle of the night wheezing, even though there are no other asthma triggers around. These are called night attacks.

◆ Sulfites: Some people have asthma attacks when they eat foods or take medicines that contain sulfites. Sulfites are chemicals used to preserve foods.

◆ Weather: Sudden changes in the weather can make asthma **symptoms** worse for some people. Just breathing in cold air can trigger an asthma attack. Other people have to avoid sudden changes in temperature. Sometimes entering a warm house after being outside on a cold day can trigger an attack.

◆ Air **pollution:** Being outdoors when the pollution levels are high can trigger an asthma attack in some people. Pollution in the air can be caused by car and truck exhaust, fires, or factories.

◆ Exercise: Some people with asthma have to avoid a lot exercise and running around, especially on days that are cold and dry. Running triggers attacks in eight out of ten children with asthma.

◆ Emotions: Some people may have an asthma attack after laughing hard, crying, or shouting. For some people, getting angry is an asthma trigger.

Some people think that high levels of air pollution can make asthma worse. They say pollution is also partly responsible for the increase in the number of children who have asthma.

Diagnosing Asthma

A number of tests must be used to help a doctor **diagnose** asthma in a person. This is partly because the **symptoms** of asthma are different in each person. One person with asthma might always have a wheezy cough. Another may have trouble breathing once in a while. Most children with asthma first sense a tight feeling in their chests.

At the doctor's

First the doctor or health care worker will weigh and measure the patient. Then they look into the patient's medical history. This history is a record of any health problems that a person has had in the past. Nearly everyone has a health record like this. It is usually kept at the person's doctor's office.

The doctor also finds out about the patient's family medical history. Asthma often runs in families. Children in these families may be **predisposed** to getting asthma. This means that if people in the patient's family have asthma, the patient is more likely to have asthma.

Once a doctor has diagnosed asthma, children can start treatment to control the symptoms and make them feel well again.

Peak flow meters measure how hard people can blow air out of their lungs. If someone cannot breathe out hard, it means his or her **airways** may be narrowed.

Testing for asthma

In one asthma test, doctors use a device called a **spirometer.** One type of spirometer is a computer "birthday cake machine." In this test, a computer screen shows a picture of a birthday cake with candles. A child being tested takes a deep breath and blows into a mouthpiece to try to "blow out" all of the candles on the screen. Then the computer measures the child's breath and figures out his or her score.

Doctors can also measure a person's breathing with a **peak flow meter.** When a person blows into the device, a marker slides up a scale. If someone's breathing level is below the normal range on the scale, it may mean that he or she has asthma. As the person's asthma improves with treatment, he or she is able to blow harder. Then the marker moves further up the scale and the peak flow scores are higher.

Treating Asthma

There are two main ways of treating asthma. The first is to treat the symptoms by taking medicine **prescribed** by a doctor. The second way is to learn what triggers asthma attacks and avoid those **triggers.**

Children with asthma can take their medicine through an inhaler that they put into their mouths. The inhaler helps them take the right amount of medicine easily.

Treating the symptoms

Several different kinds of medicines are used to treat asthma. They can be divided into two main kinds, **relievers** and **preventers.** These work in different ways, but both are usually taken by the same method. The medicines are inhaled, or breathed in. **Inhalers** are a very good way of taking asthma medicine. The medicine goes straight to where it is needed—the **airways** inside the **lungs.**

Reliever medicines are medicines people take to stop, or relieve, the symptoms of an asthma attack. Relievers work quickly to loosen the muscles around the airways. As the muscles relax, the airways become wider. Air is able to pass through more easily and it becomes easier for a person to breathe again. If they are having asthma symptoms, people with mild asthma will usually feel better after they take a couple of puffs from a reliever inhaler.

Everyone's asthma is different. Some people may only need to use reliever medicines, while others need to use both reliever and preventer medicines.

Preventer medicines have to be taken on a regular schedule because they work over a long period of time. They don't help if someone is already having an asthma attack. Preventer medicines help the airways become less **inflamed** over time. When the airways are less inflamed, they are less likely to react badly when they come in contact with an asthma trigger.

Side effects

Almost all medicines can have **side effects.** That means they can do things you weren't expecting. In some people, some asthma medicines may make them feel dizzy or like they might throw up. If you have a friend with asthma and he or she doesn't feel well after taking medicine, you should tell an adult right away.

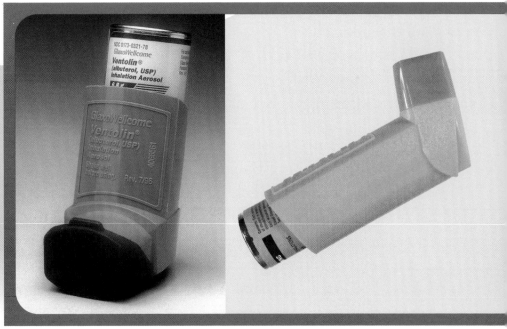

Reliever inhalers and preventer inhalers are usually different colors. This helps people see which is which. This is important because they may need to grab a reliever quickly if they have an asthma attack.

Identifying triggers

To avoid asthma **triggers,** people with asthma first have to find out what their triggers are. Some asthma triggers are easy to spot. You might have a friend or classmate who always starts wheezing or coughing after being around a dog. But sometimes it can be hard to find out what brings on an asthma attack.

A good way for people to discover what causes their asthma attacks is to keep a diary that records when their asthma **symptoms** get worse. They can record the time of day, what they've just been doing or eating, and where they have been. After a while, a pattern might appear. For example, it may become clear that an asthma attack always happens while they are outside on cold winter days. Or, it might happen after visiting a friend's house where a cat lives.

Asthma can be very tricky. No matter how much a person keeps track of things in an asthma diary, he or she still might not be able to identify a trigger for every asthma attack.

It's important for a child with asthma to talk to their doctor about how they've been feeling. They need to work together to help control the child's asthma.

People with asthma need to have regular checkups to find out how they're doing. The doctor will check to make sure the person's throat and **lungs** are all right and to see if they've been taking their medicine correctly. They will also talk about the person's asthma, and whether it has been better or worse.

Early warning signs

People with asthma need to be able to recognize an attack when it first starts. This way, they can treat it right away. Their doctors can help them learn what to look for. Here are some signs that a person might be having an asthma attack:

- becoming out of breath more easily than usual

- feeling upset for no reason

- feeling overheated even though the temperature hasn't changed

- breathing faster when they haven't been exercising

- getting tired more easily than usual

- coughing, sneezing, or clearing their throats frequently

- noises and wheezing sounds in their throats or chests when they are breathing

Classmates with Asthma

Every person's asthma is different. You might have a classmate who has mild asthma. He or she might only need to use a **reliever inhaler** once or twice a week. They can also do some exercising at recess without having any **symptoms.** These students rarely miss school because of their asthma.

Some of your friends might have to use their reliever inhalers three or more times a week. These classmates have moderate asthma. They need to use a **preventer** inhaler or other medicine regularly. These children cough or wheeze when they exercise, and they often have symptoms that wake them at night or make them miss school.

Some classmates might have severe asthma. They can't exercise without wheezing, and at night they often wake up with asthma symptoms. They also miss school because of their asthma. Sometimes they even end up in the hospital because of their asthma attacks.

Running in gym class may be too much activity for some children with asthma, but fine for others. If teachers know that a student has asthma, they can help in case of an asthma attack.

Some students who have asthma can't share lunches with other classmates. They have to be careful of what they eat to avoid triggering an asthma attack.

At school

For most of your classmates with asthma, school life isn't affected. The key to keeping asthma under control at school is by taking medicines at the right time. Most students with asthma take their inhalers to school and keep them nearby at all times. Others keep their inhalers in the school nurse's office. They make sure teachers and physical education instructors know about their asthma so everyone is prepared in case of an asthma attack.

Ordinary foods that don't bother most people can cause an asthma attack in some classmates who have asthma. These students must be careful to avoid eating foods that are asthma **triggers.** This might mean that they can't eat some of the foods served in the school cafeteria.

You might notice that a friend is taking medicines at different times than before. That's because his or her medicine schedule might change depending on the season and on how well their asthma is being controlled.

Team sports are good for people with asthma. If they have a bad day, they can always play in a position that doesn't require as much running.

Asthma and sports

Exercise is good for everyone, including people with asthma. The more physically fit a person is, the better his or her **lungs** work. For people with asthma, being fit usually means they have fewer problems with their asthma. Regular exercise to improve fitness is just as important for asthma sufferers as it is for you.

Most children with mild asthma can take part in almost any school sport or activity that they like. Swimming is great for all people, especially children with asthma. It exercises the entire body and increases breathing ability. It's especially helpful for asthma sufferers if it's done in an indoor pool because the air there is warm and moist. This kind of air doesn't irritate sensitive **airways** as much as cold, dry air does.

On days when they don't feel up to a lot of exercise, children with asthma figure out other things to do with their friends. These might include hobbies such as cooking or stamp collecting, or playing video games or chess.

School trips and vacations

Most children have their asthma under control in their daily lives. But what about when they go away on a school field trip or a vacation?

That's usually not a big problem. Everyone should make a checklist of what they'll need when they go away. You probably do this because it helps make sure you don't forget anything important. It's just the same for children with asthma, except that **inhalers** and other medicines should be at the top of their lists.

Summer camp

Many organizations sponsor summer camps for children with asthma all over the United States. At these camps, children can enjoy all of the activities and fun of summer camps while learning how to manage their asthma.

Where a person is going can affect his or her asthma. For example, a school trip to a museum in a busy city might make some of your classmates' asthma worse due to high levels of air **pollution.** And a visit to a nature preserve during **pollen** season may also **trigger** an attack. The key is to be prepared.

With some thought and planning, children with asthma will have no problem enjoying school trips and vacations away from home.

It's important for a person who is having an asthma attack to stay calm and try to relax.

How You Can Help

Sometimes, even when people are very good at controlling their asthma, they may have an asthma attack. If a friend or classmate has an asthma attack, don't panic. Just follow these steps.

1. The person should use his or her **reliever inhaler** right away.

2. You should immediately tell an adult that the child is not feeling well. It is very important to do this, even if it means interrupting a teacher.

3. The person should sit down and try to stay calm. He or she may find this hard to do if they are having trouble breathing. You and other people can help them calm down by staying calm yourselves.

4. After about five or ten minutes, the reliever inhaler should have worked. By then the person should be feeling much better. Then he or she can continue with school as usual.

5. On a few occasions, a reliever inhaler might not be enough. Then the child should see a doctor who can help get the asthma under control.

Having a classmate with asthma visit

How can you help a friend with asthma avoid having an asthma attack when they visit?

- Make sure your friend brings all of his or her medicines.

- Ask your friend to tell you and your parents what **triggers** their asthma. For example, your friend might tell you that he or she can't use a feather pillow or a sleeping bag.

- Also ask your friend to tell you and your parents what to do in case he or she has an asthma attack.

- Make sure any furry or feathered pets are kept out of the rooms where your friend will sleep or spend a lot of time.

- Make sure you and your parents know what foods could cause a problem for your friend so you don't mistakenly serve or offer them.

- Make sure you and your friend aren't in a room where someone is smoking. Cigarette smoke is bad for everyone and is a common cause of asthma attacks.

Sometimes you may need to stay indoors when spending time with a friend who has asthma.

Visiting a Friend with Asthma

For people with asthma, making small changes around the home can make life much more comfortable.

Pets

About half of children who have asthma find that pets **trigger** their **symptoms. Allergens** are found in animal fur, feathers, saliva, and skin. This means that even pets like birds can cause problems for some people with asthma. For most people whose asthma is brought on by contact with animals, it may be best not to have a pet at all. But some of your classmates may find that they can have pets as long as they take certain steps.

◆ They keep dogs, cats, and birds out of their bedrooms.

◆ They keep dogs and cats out of the house as much as possible. They also keep birds in a room where they don't spend a lot of time.

◆ Someone else in the family washes dogs and cats once or twice a month with an odor-free soap.

◆ Someone else changes cat litter boxes and the paper in birdcages every day.

While you can't play with fish like you can a dog or cat, fish are often good pets for children who have asthma.

22

Dust mites

No matter how much people clean, it's normal for dust mites to live in the dust that builds up in everybody's homes. Dust mites live in bedding, carpets, sofas, and even stuffed animals. For many people with asthma, dust mites and their droppings cause a lot of trouble. If you spend the night at the home of a friend who has asthma, you might notice some of the things the family has done to get rid of the problem. These include:

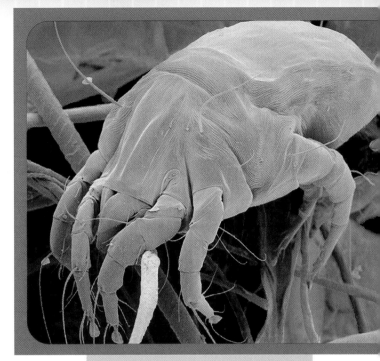

Dust mites are so small you can only see them with a microscope.

◆ removing wall-to-wall carpeting to give mites one less place to live

◆ using special covers on mattresses, pillows, and blankets to keep dust from getting into the air

◆ replacing curtains with window shades or blinds, which can be dusted more easily

◆ removing stuffed animals and other "dust-catchers" like padded chairs and shelves of knick-knacks from your friend's bedroom

◆ opening bedroom windows in cool, dry weather—dust mites don't like cold, dry air

◆ using air conditioning or dehumidifiers in the summer

◆ adding special dust filters to furnace registers

Foods

Asthma can be **triggered** by **allergies** to foods. People who have asthma will keep certain foods out of the house because they are asthma triggers, but it may be harder to avoid them when going to school or visiting friends.

Strong smells

Many people's asthma is bothered by strong smells. Often, products such as perfumes, soaps, or glue trigger their asthma. For this reason, many families choose to use soaps and other products that don't have added perfumes.

Smoking

Cigarette smoke can trigger an asthma attack. Most homes of children who have asthma are non-smoking homes. If a friend with asthma does happen to be somewhere people are smoking, they should ask people not to do it near them or go to another room.

A windy spring or summer day can blow **pollen** from trees, grasses, and flowers indoors. Because this could trigger an asthma attack, people with asthma might need to have the windows closed.

Taking care of themselves

Children with asthma must take a lot of the responsibility for taking care of their asthma themselves. Their life at home may include a routine of doing certain things to help keep it under control.

Many children keep diaries at home of their asthma **symptoms.** In their diaries, they record what medicines they are taking and how they are feeling. They may also include their readings from a **peak flow meter.** Usually, their doctors have told them what the lowest peak flow reading should be. If the peak flow reading drops below that level, it means their asthma may be getting out of control. A three-colored guide (red, yellow, and green) comes with many peak flow meters to help warn a person of an asthma attack. A reading in the red zone means he or she should seek a doctor's help to control the asthma.

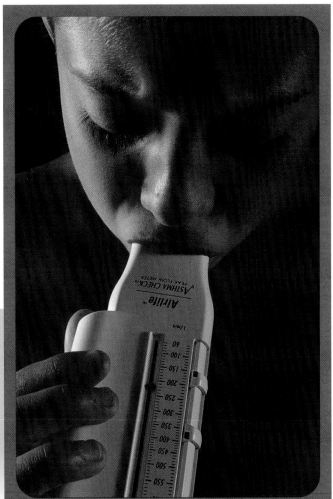

Children with asthma sometimes use a peak flow meter at home to find out if their medications are working properly, and to help them see patterns of triggers.

Asthma Success Stories

Many athletes have asthma, but they don't let it stop them from competing. Working with their doctors, many people have been able to control their asthma and become great athletes.

Debbie Meyer has suffered from asthma since childhood. But at age 16, she was the first swimmer to win three gold medals in one Olympic Games. Since then, she has broken twenty world records in swimming, and is in the Olympic Hall of Fame.

In spite of breathing difficulties, Nancy Hogshead won three gold medals and one silver medal in the 1984 Olympics. When a **bronchial** problem kept her from winning a fifth medal, a doctor discovered she had asthma. In her book, *Asthma and Exercise,* she tells about how she was diagnosed with asthma and how she learned to control her asthma with medication.

Bruce Davidson controls his asthma with medication so he can continue to ride his horse in equestrian events. He has won a silver medal and a gold medal in the Olympics as well as seven American championships and two world championships.

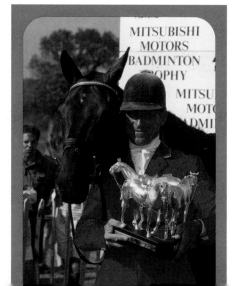

Jackie Joyner-Kersee won three Olympic gold medals in track and field events despite having severe asthma. At times she's had to use an **inhaler** to get through events, and at the 1995 USA Championship, she finished the heptathalon wearing a mask to filter out **pollen.**

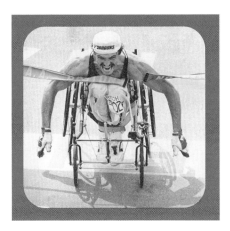

George Murray is a wheelchair marathon champion. He started racing in his wheelchair as an exercise to help control his asthma. He was the first person to break the four-minute mile in a wheelchair and the first to cross the United States in a wheelchair.

Jerome Bettis, star running back for the Pittsburgh Steelers, had asthma as a child. He has said that his parents explained to him that although he had asthma, he could do whatever he wanted to do. He believes that the key to his success was learning about his asthma early on and being able to control it.

Learning More about Asthma

The American Lung Association (ALA) was started in 1904 to fight the lung disease **tuberculosis.** Today it works to inform and treat people with all types of **conditions** that affect the respiratory system, including asthma. It offers programs and materials to teach people about asthma, and provides money to research new treatments.

The American Lung Association has 130 local Lung Associations all over the United States. You can find the address and phone number of your nearest local Lung Association by looking in the phone book or online.

You can get booklets and other information about asthma from your local Lung Association. They also have a kit to help children learn about asthma. The kit includes puzzles, posters, stickers, stories, and a board game. In addition, many local Lung Associations sponsor summer camps for children with asthma. They also hold workshops about asthma for children, parents, teachers, and other school workers.

Open Airways for Schools

Open Airways for Schools (OAS) is a program offered by the American Lung Association that teaches children ages 8 through 11 about asthma. Trained volunteers from the program visit elementary schools around the country to teach students how to identify asthma **triggers** and prevent asthma attacks.

While the OAS program is designed to help children who have asthma, children without asthma can also take part. The program uses group work, stories, and games to teach students about asthma. It teaches them how to identify asthma and how to get it under control with the help of parents, teachers, school nurses, and doctors.

The goal of OAS is to teach children in all elementary schools in the United States about asthma. As part of this goal, Open Airways for Schools in Spanish was started. Spanish-speaking volunteers teach the program in schools where there are Spanish-speaking students with asthma. This way the program can reach as many children as possible.

Glossary

airway   tube that carries air in and out of the lungs

allergen   substance that causes an allergic reaction

allergy   condition that causes a person's body to react badly to something that is harmless to most people

bronchi   two airways that branch off from the windpipe and carry air into and out of the lungs

condition   health problem that a person has for a long time, perhaps for all of his or her life

diagnose   to recognize what illness or condition a person has

environment   surroundings; everything around a person, including people, plants, animals, water, air, buildings, and towns

immune system   parts of the body, including organs and cells, that work together to defend it from infection and fight off sickness

inflamed   red, swollen, and sensitive

inhaler   device that helps people with asthma breathe in medicine

lung   organ in the chest that fills with air and is used for breathing. People have two lungs.

mucus   sticky substance made in many parts of the body that moistens and protects the linings of the nose, throat, and other areas

peak flow meter   device for measuring breathing levels; it shows how hard someone can blow air out of the lungs

pollen   tiny grains of dust that flowers release and that help make new plants

pollution   harmful substances and chemicals in the environment

predisposed   ability or likelihood of something happening. Some people are predisposed to developing asthma.

prescribe   to tell someone the kind and amount of medicine to take

preventer   kind of asthma medicine that works over a long period to soothe a person's airways so they become less sensitive

reliever   kind of asthma medicine that stops the symptoms of an asthma attack quickly

side effect   unwanted effect of a medicine

spirometer   instrument for measuring the amount of air a person can breathe out

spore   tiny part of a mold that can grow into a new mold

symptom   change in the body that is a sign of a health problem; the effect an illness or condition has on the body

trigger   anything that bothers the airways of a person with asthma and brings on asthma symptoms

tuberculosis   disease caused by bacteria that affects the lungs

More Books to Read

Cromwell, Sharon. *Why Can't I Breathe Underwater?: And Other Questions about the Respiratory System.* Chicago: Heinemann Library, 1998.

Dudley Gold, Susan. *Asthma.* Berkeley Heights, N.J.: Enslow Publishers, 2000.

O'Neill, Linda. *Imagine Having Asthma.* Vero Beach, Fla.: Rourke Press, 2000.

Parker, Steve. *The Lungs & Respiratory System.* New York: Raintree Steck-Vaughn, 1997.

Simpson, Carolyn. *Coping with Asthma.* New York: Rosen Publishing, 1999.

Weitzman, Elizabeth. *Let's Talk About Having Asthma.* New York: Rosen

Index